Published by Creative Education
P.O. Box 227, Mankato, Minnesota 56002
Creative Education is an imprint of The Creative Company.

Design and production by Stephanie Blumenthal
Printed in the United States of America

Photographs by Alamy (Pat Behnke, Tony Cordoza, Mary Evans Picture Library,
North Wind Picture Archive, Popperfoto, Visual Arts Library), Corbis (Bettmann,
Christie's Images, Stephen F. Hayes, Ramon Manent, Museum of M.D. Mallorca,
Stapleton Collection, Baldwin H. Ward & Kathryn C. Ward),
Getty Images (Tim Graham, Hulton Archive), istockphoto

Library of Congress Cataloging-in-Publication Data
Hanel, Rachael.
Knights / by Rachael Hanel.
p. cm. — (Fearsome fighters)
Includes bibliographical references and index.
ISBN-13: 978-1-58341-536-8
1. Knights and knighthood—Juvenile literature.
2. Civilization, Medieval—Juvenile literature. I. Title. II. Series.

CR4513.H37 2007
940.1—dc22   2006021843

First edition
2 4 6 8 9 7 5 3 1

KNIGHTS

RACHAEL HANEL

FEARSOME FIGHTERS

CREATIVE EDUCATION

From the beginning of time, wherever groups of people have lived together, they have also fought among themselves. Some have fought for control of basic necessities—food, water, and shelter—or territory. Others have been spurred to fight by religious differences. Still others have fought solely for sport. Throughout the ages, some fighters have taken up arms willingly; others have been forced into battle. For all, however, the ultimate goal has always been victory.

Medieval knights in Europe charged into battle seeking to conquer land for their lords and masters. Wearing heavy, shining armor, these warriors riding high atop horses canvassed the countryside, besieging castles and fortresses and meeting opposing groups of knights face-to-face in open fields, their sharp lances and swords at the ready. The clashes were violent and the warfare bloody. But both on and off the battlefield, knights upheld a way of life known as chivalry, which emphasized kindness, bravery, and respect for others. Knights and stories of their adventures soon vaulted to legendary status. It's no wonder that even today, knights and knighthood remain popular concepts idealized by authors, filmmakers, and people the world over.

FULFILLING AN IMPORTANT ROLE

Knights burst onto the scene at a time when chaos and upheaval marked European life. Up until A.D. 476, the **Roman Empire** ruled large parts of Europe, including areas such as modern-day Britain, Germany, and France. When the Roman Empire collapsed, bands of roving, uncultured tribes using brute force swept in to **plunder** treasures and conquer land for themselves. Eventually, the **nobles** of small kingdoms pushed out vandalizing tribes, and hundreds of tiny provinces emerged from the strife. Each small kingdom ruled itself; no powerful **central government** held any control.

Most people born in these isolated European kingdoms seldom ventured past the lands they knew, and people from other parts of the world rarely traveled outside of their own borders. With no trade network yet connecting Europe to Asia and Africa, and with no knowledge of the Americas, the people of Europe had

little interaction with other cultures. European villagers grew crops and took care of animals, and some served as craftsmen and blacksmiths. Everything they needed could be found within their village borders.

But the lords and nobles who ruled these lands always wanted more land, which would result in more money. They became hungry for power and wealth. To fulfill their wishes, they created informal armies that attacked neighboring lands, destroying crops and villages and making Europe an especially violent place to live. Each kingdom soon realized that the defense of its land was of the utmost importance. At first, nobles and lords hired boys into military service. The young men worked for whoever gave them the most money, and the title "knight" was bestowed upon them.

Around A.D. 900, the small kingdoms evolved into a feudal system throughout the

LIFE FOR MEDIEVAL PEASANTS WAS FULL OF HARD WORK

European countries of Britain, Germany, France, and Italy. In the feudal system, a king owned a huge tract of land. He allowed powerful lords to control sections of the land in exchange for their loyalty and support. These lords, in turn, parceled out their land to less powerful nobles, who pledged their loyalty and support to the lords. As the system grew more organized, so did the means of protection. The military army of young boys turned into a more formal knighthood. Each lord who wanted to protect his land employed knights—no longer boys, but professional fighters—in his service. In exchange for a piece of land to rule over and sometimes his own castle, a knight pledged to protect the lord and his land. The knight was given direct control over the land he was allotted as well as the peasants who lived there farming and tending the animals. The peasants were required to turn over most of their food and income to the knight and his lord. In exchange, they received a piece of land, a home in which to live, and protection in times of war.

As lords' tracts of land grew larger and larger, they needed extra protection, since their wealth and holdings looked ever more attractive to people wanting to add to their own riches. Fortunately, the wealthier and more powerful a lord was, the better he could afford stronger, swifter, and more organized knights. A rich lord might have dozens of knights in his service.

A KNIGHT WHO WAS LOYAL TO HIS LORD (ABOVE) NEVER HAD TO WORRY ABOUT GOING HUNGRY

$\mathcal{K}$nights generally ate well. They needed to be quick and strong, so a lord was sure to provide them with plenty of food. A knight's diet consisted mostly of meat—deer, boar, peacock, and chicken. Cooks added other foods, such as garlic, onions, and mustard to flavor the meat. Spices such as pepper, cloves, ginger, and nutmeg were considered exotic because they came from faraway lands, and only the richest lords could afford them. Knights ate plenty of fish as well, since meat was forbidden on Church holy days. Thick bread was served at most meals, but vegetables were not common.

Knights were expected to ride into battle whenever their lord commanded and might spend months or years away from home. When knights were at home, they spent time with their families and supervised the peasants and other workers of the **manor**, including blacksmiths, swordsmiths, and caretakers. Knights married, but rarely for love. Instead, marriage was a union used to benefit the knight's status and was usually arranged by a lord. The lord might offer his own daughter or another close relative to a knight. Because a knight had to pay for his own armor and weapons, he wanted to marry a wealthy woman. That way, he had a better chance of receiving a nice home or quality battle supplies. The lord might even include prime pieces of land as part of the marriage union.

A knight's wife held important duties. When her husband was away in battle, she was responsible for the home and the manor. She sometimes had to defend the home herself. It was

also her job to bear the knight's children. A knight wanted many children and especially hoped for a son to whom he could pass down land and valuable weapons. A knight's son likely would also become a knight.

At home with their families, knights entertained themselves in many ways. One popular pastime involved listening to minstrels. Minstrels traveled from manor to manor, country to country, singing, playing instruments, and telling stories, such as epic romances, through song. They provided the only source of news from one country to another, although news often took months and even years to reach faraway destinations. Knights also played games such as chess, which honed their strategic skills for battle. They hunted, using trained hawks or falcons to swoop down on small prey, and chased other wild game such as bears, deer, and wolves in the forests outside the manor walls.

The most important aspect of a knight's

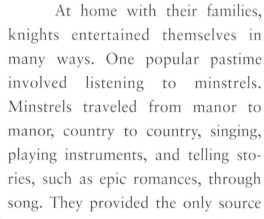

Jousting was a dangerous part of knights' training

When knights weren't on the battlefield, they participated in tournaments to show off their **jousting** and battle skills for their adoring public. Some tournaments lasted several days and attracted crowds from far and wide, along with merchants who hoped to sell their wares to the public. Knights enjoyed the tournaments because the competitions provided them a chance to keep their fighting skills sharp. Also, a winning knight could claim the armor, weapons, and horses of the knights he defeated, making him a wealthier man. Even though these tournaments were supposed to be lighthearted, knights sometimes became aggressive, and some were killed.

life was to behave in a chivalrous manner. Chivalry told a knight how to act. It meant using good manners and being kind. Knights were expected to uphold the rights of all people, live a good life, and protect the weak. In battle, knights were to be brave, loyal, and willing to die for their lord. Perhaps most importantly, chivalry held that knights were to act courteously toward women, a practice that stemmed from the Catholic tradition of worshipping and honoring the Virgin Mary, the mother of Jesus Christ; most Europeans, including knights, practiced Catholicism.

Chivalry was an especially important concept to the Catholic Church, which promoted the values of kindness and respect and served as the **moral** influence for all of Europe. In the early days of knighthood, church officials despised the violent ways in which knights acted. But church leaders soon saw the strong bonds of brotherhood that formed among knights and hoped that knights would carry their chivalrous ideals to the general population.

Because of the knights' actions and lifestyle, people throughout Europe held them in high regard. People also respected knights because knighthood and wealth were closely tied together. In order to gain an advantage in battle, a knight had to buy his own weapons, equipment, and horses. Thus, the most successful knights were often the richest. In time, knights became a high-ranking class. Weak men, lords, and even kings deferred to them for protection in times of war.

As the Middle Ages progressed and warfare evolved, knights adapted their armor accordingly

SLASHING THEIR WAY TO VICTORY

There was no mistaking a knight when he appeared on the battlefield. At his side, he carried prominent, intimidating weapons—a sharp, long sword and a smaller knife. The most successful knights sat high atop strong, graceful horses that galloped thunderously across the countryside. A knight's most defining feature, though, was his shining suit of armor, which covered him from head to toe. The armor—made from either iron or steel—made breathing difficult and movement cumbersome. But the knight wore it because it was the only thing that protected him from the vicious weapons wielded by his enemies.

Armor on early knights consisted of nothing more than linen cloth waxed or oiled into a hardened shell. Later, **chain mail** (known simply as mail before the 18th century) became the armor of choice for the warring knight. Creating chain mail involved tedious work for the village blacksmith, who had to form and link together thousands of tiny iron rings. The chain mail links protected a knight from heavy weapon blows, and because they were small, they made for a flexible uniform that gracefully draped over a knight's body. A chain mail suit consisted of a knee-length shirt (a hauberk) or a waist-length shirt (a habergeon). A knight wore chain mail socks known as chausses, mittens called mitons, and a hood, or coif.

As time passed, knights discovered that chain mail didn't always offer adequate protection. As a result, iron and steel solid plate armor appeared in the 1300s. Solid armor better protected a knight from armies that began using arrows, whose sharp and narrow tips glided through chain mail's iron rings. Knights still wore chain mail, but they now wore it underneath armor. A full suit of armor consisted of several pieces, among them shin guards, thigh

Medieval chain mail is displayed in museums today

guards, breast plates, arm guards, and shoulder guards. No part of a knight's body went uncovered. Only small eye slits or a hole in front of the mouth provided any ventilation. Because a suit of armor quickly became stifling, a knight waited until the very last minute to put it on. Assistants had to help him into the armor, as the full suit weighed upwards of 55 pounds (25 kg). A knight also used a shield, a solid piece of iron or steel held in front of him, to protect himself from weapon blows.

Knightly weaponry was designed to puncture or destroy chain mail or a suit of armor. Knights used a variety of swords, spears, arrows, and heavy weapons on the battlefield. A knight's chief weapon was his lance, a long, pointed spike held underneath the arm. The lance was considered a thrusting device; that is, it was shoved into an opponent, not thrown, as its weight made it unsuitable for throwing. A knight tucked his lance under his arm while riding his horse and aimed the pointed weapon at the weakest areas of his opponents' armor—usually anywhere two pieces of armor came together, such as at the knee or shoulder. A galloping horse and strong knight threw much power behind a lance thrust, and the resulting bodily injury was often deadly.

Knights also carried with them slashing swords. These were created for hand-to-hand combat after a knight dismounted his horse. In the early **Middle Ages**, the sword was flat and double-edged, or sharp on both edges. However, the sword soon evolved into a diamond shape, with its four sides coming to a pointed end; this was to more easily pierce through chain mail or gaps in armor. The handle of a sword sometimes contained a relic of a saint that the knight hoped would grant him special protection. This relic might be a lock of hair, a piece of clothing, or a bone fragment. A dagger was a shorter sword also used for inflicting slashing wounds. The dagger's size allowed it to fit between plates of armor or through a helmet's vulnerable vision slits.

Large, heavy weapons allowed knights to crush armor instead of piercing it. Knights used the power of a mace—a metal pole that held a large, heavy ball at the end—to smash through armor. Its weight meant the mace inflicted serious, quick

A FULL SUIT OF ARMOR MADE MOVEMENT DIFFICULT

*Creating plate armor was not easy. The task, which could take several weeks, fell to a village's armorer and his assistants. First, the men heated iron to a high temperature. Then they molded each plate using a hammer. The armorer joined the plates together with tiny **rivets** and leather straps. To test the armor's strength, the creator fired an arrow into the metal. He knew he had a good suit when the arrow dented the armor but didn't pierce it. A metal suit might cost one-quarter of a knight's annual income, but good armor paid off on the battlefield.*

injury. A similar weapon, the flail, which featured a heavy ball attached to a pole by a chain, could also strike an opponent with great force.

Cannons and guns were introduced in the 1500s, and the use of these types of mechanical weapons required great skill. In the early days, cannons and guns were not very accurate and often backfired, injuring those who used them. The force behind these weapons meant that even a knight's strong armor could not protect him from injury.

While a knight's armor and weapons served important roles on the battlefield, his most treasured asset was his trusty companion—his horse. Without a strong steed to carry him into battle, a knight was weak. A knight with his armor might weigh 250 to 300 pounds (115–135 kg); a horse needed to steadily bear that weight. Because knights needed powerful horses, they often bred the animals purposely to achieve desired results. A strong horse was called a destrier and might weigh twice as much as a conventional riding horse. A heavy horse also gave a knight more power behind his lance thrust. A knight's horse might wear horseshoes clad with short spikes to inflict serious injury if it stepped on an opponent. The horse also wore protective armor over vulnerable areas, such as its chest, torso, back, and head.

Another important factor on the battlefield was a knight's heraldry. Heraldry was a system of colorful symbols that distinguished knights from one another. Once a knight dressed in full armor and put on his helmet, he looked like any other knight. In order to prevent knights from killing their allies in battle, a system of colors and designs was put into place. The designs might feature animals such as falcons or bears, or mythical creatures such as dragons and unicorns. All heraldry boasted bright colors—blues, purples, reds, and greens. Knights wore heraldry on their helmets or shields and on coats that covered their armor, and carried banners that featured their heraldry into battle. A knight's tomb might be covered with his heraldry. The heraldry was passed down from generation to generation, with sons adding a slight change each time. Men called heralds kept track of the different designs to ensure that no two families used the same heraldry. Because they knew the different knights by their logos, heralds were responsible for getting messages to knights on the battlefield and identifying those who died.

MEDIEVAL DOCTORS OFFERED LIMITED CARE FOR WOUNDS

A knight was subjected to a host of injuries on the battlefield. The pierce of a sword might result in a quick and relatively painless death. But if he was injured, a knight might suffer in agony. Without painkilling drugs (which were not yet invented), the treatment was often just as painful as the initial blow. Doctors sealed open wounds with a hot iron or boiling oil, and pincers were used to pry arrowheads from flesh. Even with treatment, an infected wound might eventually require the amputation of a limb and could even lead to death.

FIGTHTING FOR THEIR LORD

Knights fought on a number of different fronts. They might stay close to home and fight a neighboring lord and his knights through a series of small battles. Or they might band together with neighboring warriors, unite under their king with numbers in the hundreds or thousands, and fight knights from other countries. Sometimes, as in the Crusades, knights might travel thousands of miles and participate in gigantic and complex wars that lasted hundreds of years.

In any case, a knight's training started when he was young and lasted several years. Around the age of seven, a boy born of a knight or other high-class parents was sent away to live with his father's master or a powerful relative. The young knight-in-training was considered a page. He ran errands, served food, and performed other duties for the nobleman and the woman of the manor. In exchange for his services, the page received a good education. He learned to read and write, play music, and observe good manners. His preparations for later fighting also started, as he was taught how to care for horses and learned a little about weaponry and fighting techniques by watching others or practicing with supervision.

Around the age of 13, the page became a squire. Squires studied directly with a knight and received more rigorous training for knighthood. They learned how to use weapons and participated in mock battles. At the same time, they continued their servitude, helping the knight in various tasks, including cleaning weapons and taking care of horses. Sometimes a squire rode into battle to

YOUNG SQUIRES (ABOVE) WERE EVENTUALLY KNIGHTED IN ELABORATE AND RITUALISTIC CEREMONIES (OPPOSITE)

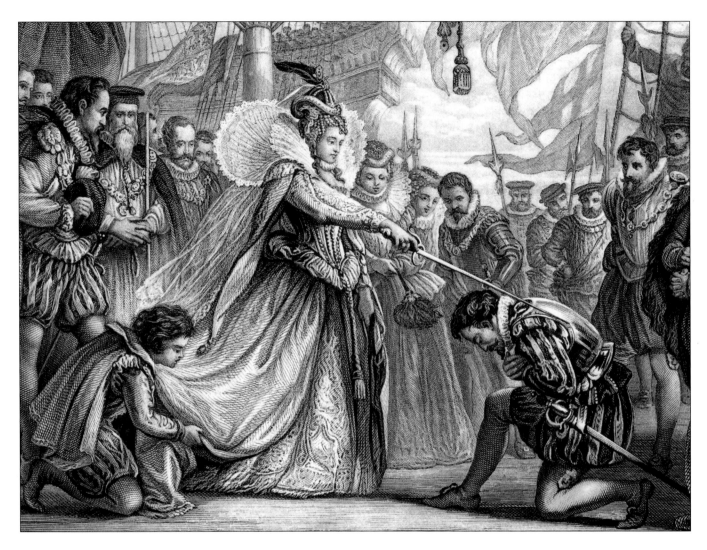

attend to and observe his knight.

Between the ages of 18 and 21, with his training satisfactorily completed, the squire became a knight in an elaborate ceremony. The night before the ceremony, the squire took a cleansing bath and quietly prayed to God for guidance. The next morning, dressed all in white, the prospective knight came before his lord and teacher. A priest blessed him and his sword. Women close to the lord's family led the knight away and helped him dress in full armor. He then returned to the ceremonial hall to be formally knighted. The lord took a sword and gently

tapped the young man three times on the shoulder, proclaiming him a knight. Then the lord tucked the knight's sword into a belt, buckled it onto the knight, and gave him a new pair of spurs. From that moment on, the knight was to remain faithful to his lord throughout his life.

Once a knight completed his training, he, along with the other knights of the manor, could be called into battle at any time. In battle, a knight's overall strategy was to fight until the enemy was weakened, dead, or forced to surrender because he didn't want to see more death. Sometimes this took days or weeks. Other times,

*T*he most famous battles in which knights fought were known as the Crusades. The Crusades lasted for two centuries, fought in waves from 1095 to 1291. During the Crusades, European knights sought to reclaim the **Holy Land** for Christians from the Muslims who dominated the area. The European knights grew concerned when Christians making pilgrimages to the place of Jesus's life and death were attacked by Muslims. At various times, the Christian knights were successful in defeating the Muslims. At other times, the Muslims successfully defended their holdings. To this day, the majority of the Middle East is comprised of Muslim populations.

battles were quick and deadly.

When knights fought against neighboring manors, the most common battle technique was to lay **siege** to the enemy castle. If knights didn't encounter any resistance, they might ruin crops and kill animals. This left villagers without food and the lord without any income. The lord might not have any choice but to surrender to the conquering knights and give his land to their lord.

Sometimes, though, knights encountered resistance from willful villagers when they tried to lay siege to a castle or manor. In this case, knights might surround the castle or manor and prevent anyone from leaving. Occasionally, brave villagers might ride outside the manor's walls to confront knights in hand-to-hand combat. Most often, though, the lord, his family, and the villagers remained trapped within the walls. To further the attack, knights launched rocks or other weapons at the walls via **catapults**. This weakened the walls and could cause bodily injury. After a time, those inside ran out of food or became sick and were unable to defend themselves any longer.

AN ESTIMATED NINE MILLION PEOPLE—CHRISTIANS AND MUSLIMS—WERE KILLED DURING THE CRUSADES

At times, knights fought on a battlefield, either near or far from home. When war was imminent, opposing knights agreed to meet at a certain time and let the victorious party lay claim to land and riches for its lord. Planning for battle took much effort. A king or lord sent word to all of his subjects requesting help. The knights of each lord came together to prepare for battle and sometimes enlisted the help of peasants and villagers. Knights readied their armor,  weapons, and horses, while peasants and villagers gathered food and supplies and armed themselves with axes and long, pointed poles. Messengers let everyone know when and where the clash would take place.

At the appointed time, the two armies gathered on opposite sides of the battlefield. On each side stood a line of mounted knights, their polished armor glinting in the daylight. Squires accompanied the knights, and sometimes even the king or lord himself would stand at the very back of the army, shouting directions and giving commands.

At a signal—a hand movement or the sound of a trumpet—the two groups charged toward each other at full speed. With their lances held straight out, the knights formed an imposing, moving wall of deadly spikes. As they came together in the middle of the field, the knights tried to deliver a fatal lance blow upon their enemies. Occasionally, the power behind two knights charging toward each other at full speed caused their lances to clash with such force that they shattered. In this case, the knights dismounted and drew out their smaller swords and daggers for hand-to-hand combat. Those knights whose lances remained intact stayed on their horses, trying to kill or knock down as many opponents as possible.

Sometimes, an army of knights opted not to charge, instead lying in wait. By doing so, the knights tried to trick their opponents into believing that they were unprepared. Thus, their oppo-

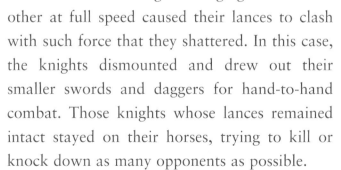

CONDITIONS IN MEDIEVAL HOMES WERE CROWDED AND OFTEN DIRTY, BUT KNIGHTS AND LORDS ATE WELL

$\mathcal{K}$nights did not live in a particularly clean society. Medieval life lacked the type of sanitation that we're used to today. In towns and manor villages, people dumped their waste into the streets. Dirty water—a byproduct of materials used in blacksmith and dye shops—also made its way into the public streets. Animals roamed around loose in public areas, as most villagers had just a small plot of land and let their animals forage for food wherever they could find it. It was up to homeowners to keep the streets clean, but they had little incentive to do so, and the filth accumulated.

nents would be lured toward them and the long, wooden poles, sharpened to a point, that they hid at their feet. Right before the opposing line reached them, the knights grabbed the pointy spears and raised them up, injuring or killing the horses and the men they carried.

Toward the later Middle Ages, around 1300, skilled archers began to help knights on the battlefield. Kneeling behind a protective wall or some other type of barrier, they launched their arrows high into the air at the enemy. These fighters became more important in battle as time wore on, as did men who were well-versed in the mechanics of operating cannons and guns, introduced around 1500.

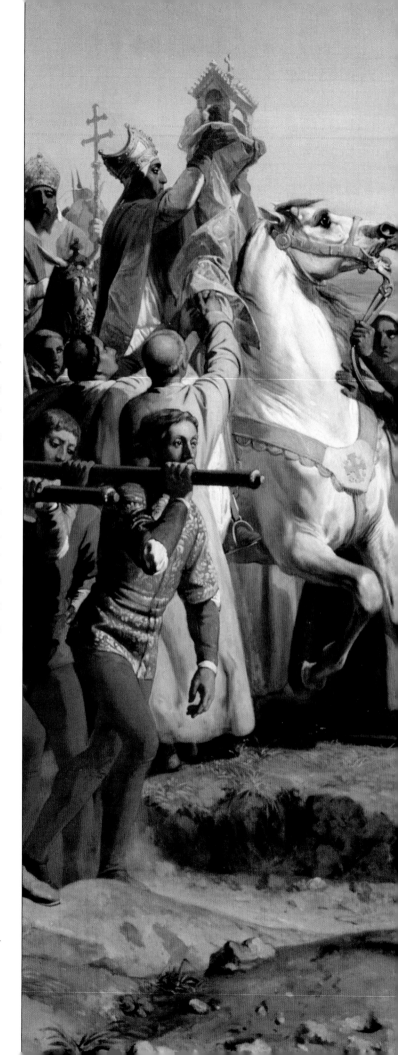

ARCHERS WERE OFTEN AN ARMY'S FIRST LINE OF OFFENSE

THE BRAVEST AND THE BEST

Knights' brave and gallant efforts on battlefields earned them a lofty place in society. Stories of their exploits spread from one region to another, sometimes embellished in a way that transformed knights into legends. Although they fought several centuries ago, stories of knights' heroic deeds and battlefield successes live on to make them popular figures yet today.

One well-known knight was William Marshal (1147–1219) of England. Marshal was a younger son, which meant that he would not inherit his father's land, since that right was reserved for a family's eldest son. Instead, Marshal's family sent him away to train as a knight. He achieved knighthood in 1167. Marshal and his army became distinguished for their undefeated record in battlefield tournaments—in which knights jousted with each other in front of audiences—and Marshal quickly gained the public's favor.

In fact, Marshal's fighting style so impressed Eleanor of Aquitaine (c. 1122–1204), the wife of England's King Henry II (1133–89), that he was appointed head of the royal military of her son, Prince Henry (1155–83), in 1170. When Prince Henry died in 1183, Marshal joined the Crusades. Upon his return, he served as chief knight and confidant to King Henry II.

Marshal is an example of a knight who married for power and riches. He married Isabel de Clare (c. 1174–1220), the daughter of a powerful nobleman, and became the owner of vast tracts of land and a magnificent estate. He also gained the title of **earl** of Pembroke. Marshal was said to have acted with great chivalry, always remaining loyal to his master and acting in gentlemanly ways. He continued to fight as a knight even into old age. At the age of 70, he was credited with leading the defeat of Philip II (1165–1223) of France, thereby securing land for the British.

WILLIAM MARSHAL PERSONIFIED THE IDEAL KNIGHT

*T*he original "knight in shining armor" is considered to be St. George (c. 275–303). According to tradition, George was a Christian soldier in the Roman Empire. He was tortured for his Christian beliefs and executed. Afterwards, he was viewed as a **martyr**, and many people were inspired to convert to Christianity because of his courage in standing up for what he believed in even as death loomed. George's legend grew after he died; he was said to have slain a dragon to save a princess from certain death. The tales surrounding St. George embody the ideas of chivalry and bravery that were later found among knights.

Another famous English knight was Edward the Black Prince (1330–76), eldest son of King Edward III (1312–77) of England. The Black Prince—who perhaps got his name from the black coat he wore over his armor—exhibited bravery on several battlefields during the Hundred Years' War (1337–1453), during which England tried to make France part of its territory. In 1346, at the age of 16, Edward led the English to victory at the battle of Crécy in France. Ten years later, at the French battle of Poitiers, Edward captured France's King John II (1319–64). Honoring the knightly code, he treated his captive with respect and kindness. King John II was released after agreeing to treaties with England, including one that gave the region of Aquitaine in southwestern France to the British. Edward later became prince of Aquitaine.

In 1366, Edward went to the battle of Najera, in present-day Spain, to support Peter the Cruel (1334–69), who ruled over the Spanish kingdoms of Castile and León but was under attack from his brother, Henry (1334–79), who also wanted control of the region. Edward's motto was *ich dien*, German for "I serve," a phrase he took from a **Bohemian** king who died in the battle of Crécy. Edward admired the fact that the king rode into battle even though he was blind, and he decided to use the king's motto as a sign of respect.

Two storied knights who changed history: Edward the Black Prince (above) and St. George (opposite)

Although only men could officially become knights, women at times acted as knights or even dressed as men in order to fight in battles. The young French woman Joan of Arc (1412–31) is the most famous example of a female who acted as a knight. Joan was born in a French village, the daughter of a farmer. At the time, France was still entangled in the Hundred Years' War against England. As a young girl, Joan claimed she saw visions from God that told her to drive the British out of France. She gained the confidence of the future French king, Charles VII (1403–61), and he granted her permission to ride into Orléans—the site of a major battle—as a knight. He outfitted her with the best armor, weapons, and a horse, as she was too poor to afford the equipment herself.

When Joan entered Orléans, it looked as if the French would meet sure defeat. However, roles soon reversed, and the French held off the English forces. Joan's exact role in the battle is not known. At the very least, she served to boost the morale of the French knights. At most, she may have used skilled military tactics and strategy to secure the French victory. Joan was said to

THE REVERED JOAN OF ARC (LEFT); EARLIER FRENCH
KNIGHTS IN THE CRUSADES (OPPOSITE)

S ome knights focused on caring for the weak and sick. The Knights of St. John, later known as the Hospitallers, were originally French monastic knights who cared for ill and tired pilgrims on their way to and from the Holy Land. They later became active in defending the Holy Land during the Crusades. Another group, the Order of Teutonic Knights, was formed in the early 12th century to aid **Prussian** knights injured during the Crusades. The order was powerful through the 1300s, but it then fizzled out. It reorganized in the late 20th century to perform religious and charitable work.

have been wounded in battle but pulled an arrow out of her arm to continue her charge. She was later captured by the English, put on trial for **heresy**, and burned at the stake at the age of 19. In 1920, she was declared a saint by Pope Benedict XV (1854–1922).

While some kings preferred to send their knights into battle, other kings actively participated in fights as knights themselves. One such king was Richard the Lionhearted (1157–99), king of England and another son of Henry II and Eleanor of Aquitaine. King Richard was a prominent figure in the Third Crusade. He joined forces with Philip II of France and traveled to the Holy Land in 1190. There, the two leaders attacked the city of Acre (in modern-day Israel) in an attempt to drive out Muslim forces. Richard tricked the Muslim king, Saladin (c. 1137–93), by telling him that if he turned Acre over to the Christians, Richard would free the inhabitants of the city. Saladin agreed, but Richard didn't follow through on his promise. Instead, he ignored chivalric code and ordered hundreds of Muslims to be slaughtered. Richard ultimately failed in his battle to take Jerusalem, but Saladin did agree to a truce, which made it easier for Christian pilgrims to pass through the Holy Land without harassment from Muslims.

After leaving the Holy Land, Richard was captured while on his way through Austria. He spent two years as a prisoner of the Germans, until his family paid a sizable **ransom** for his return to England. There, he earned the nickname "heart of the lion" for his courage and bravery on the battlefield as he crushed an attempt by his brother John (c. 1166–1216) to take over the crown and gained back lands in France that were lost during his captivity. Richard was killed in battle in 1199 while laying siege to a castle in France, seeking to capture the treasures within its walls. An arrow pierced his shoulder, and the subsequent infection proved deadly. His remains were buried in France.

KING RICHARD THE LIONHEARTED WAS KNOWN FOR HIS IMMENSE COURAGE—AND OCCASIONAL RUTHLESSNESS—IN BATTLE

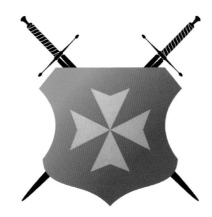

THE LEGENDS LIVE ON

The effectiveness of knights on the battlefield began to decline around 1500 as more battles incorporated the use of cannons and guns. Cannonballs and bullets more easily penetrated a knight's armor than did spears and swords. Without the protection of armor, a knight became nearly useless. At the same time, archers became more important fighters. Arrows launched from their **longbows** flew at high speeds toward the enemy and were more effective than a knight's cumbersome hand-to-hand combat with swords. **Mercenaries** also increasingly replaced knights, especially as wars lasted years and years. Since they were paid solely to fight, mercenaries could spend as much time as necessary on the battlefield. Knights, who had land and family responsibilities at home, did not like being away for long periods of time.

As knights found themselves called into battle less frequently, they spent more time taking care of matters at home. They watched over their families and the peasants who worked their land, and enforced law and order. Despite the fact that they rarely went to battle anymore, knights remained respected members of society and held on to their titles.

By the 16th century, feudalism itself was on the decline. One reason for this was that kings had little land to give away anymore. Land instead stayed within families, passed down from generation to generation. Also, kings no longer relied on knights for protection as national armies emerged. Battlefield jousting became nothing more than simple entertainment.

Even though knights no longer ruled the battlefields, the notions of bravery and chivalry remained intact. Men who exhibited these positive characteristics were still knighted and revered by the public. The Catholic Church also continued to promote these ideals, and organiza-

KNIGHTS LIVED ON IN WESTERN CULTURE THROUGH ARTWORK

tions of men who embraced a knight's positive characteristics formed.

Knights still exist today, although the title is now solely ceremonial. In Britain, people who have made positive contributions to the country are granted knighthood. Famous musicians such as Elton John and Paul McCartney hold the title of knight. The reigning king or queen performs the ceremony, which involves a tap on the shoulder with a sword, just as in centuries past. After the ceremony, men receive the title of "sir" and women are titled "dame." The formal title is Knight Commander of the Most Excellent Order of the British Empire.

In France, one can be inducted as a chevalier (knight) in the French Legion of Honor. The Legion can hold a maximum of 113,425 knights and is about 80 percent full today. In 1998, all surviving veterans of World War I who had served on French soil—no matter their country of origin—were made Knights of the Legion. These knights wear an honorary badge on a ribbon on the left side of their chests.

Even those who have not been knighted can today relive the era of knights and chivalry through events called renaissance festivals. At these festivals, men dress up in full armor and compete in mock battles complete with horses,

QUEEN ELIZABETH II AND SIR PAUL MCCARTNEY (ABOVE)

$\mathcal{V}$isitors today can tour William Marshal's great castle, located in the town of Pembroke in southwest Wales. The castle was founded in 1093, and Marshal took control of it in 1189 as earl of Pembroke. Pembroke Castle is surrounded on three sides by the River Cleddau, which provided excellent protection from intruders. When Marshal first moved to the castle, it was made of wood and earth, but he supervised the construction of a mighty stone fortification. Towers flank the castle, from which soldiers once peered down and shot at enemy invaders.

swords, and various weapons. The festivals often incorporate elements from medieval life, including recreated villages and people dressed like anyone from common villagers to noble ladies. Musicians wander about, singing and playing instruments. Even the food is authentic to the medieval lifestyle. Entering a renaissance festival village is like stepping back in time.

Another way to travel back to the time of knighthood is to read one of the many novels written about knightly exploits or to watch one of the countless films memorializing knights. For hundreds of years, knights' adventures have captured the imagination, making for **romanticized** stories in which men behave in gallant, kind, and heroic ways. Spanish author Miguel de Cervantes was the first writer to explore the fascinating world of knighthood in a popular novel. The title character of his 1605 book *Don Quixote* is a man enchanted by stories of knights. He decides to become a knight himself, seeking to correct the world's wrongs in his travels through Spain.

Just over 200 years after the publication of *Don Quixote*, public interest in knighthood and the Middle Ages was again piqued by Scottish novelist Sir Walter Scott's book *Ivanhoe*. The book, set in 12th-century England, follows the adventures of Wilfred of Ivanhoe, a nobleman who has come back from fighting in the Crusades. Richard the Lionhearted plays a role in the book, which accurately tells the story of his imprisonment and return to England.

Perhaps the most famous knight tales ever told are of the great King Arthur. Stories about King Arthur embody the characteristics of a fair and proper man and first emerged in Britain around A.D. 600. Historians today still debate whether or not King Arthur was a real person. Some believe he lived in the fifth or sixth century and helped the early British fight the **Saxons**. One legendary account says that he single-handedly killed more than 900 men. Others think his character is based on a ruling member of the Roman Empire. Or, he may have evolved from a god worshiped by the **Celts**. On the other hand, he may have no historical basis at all. Rather, his exploits could have been a combination of many war leadership stories.

In any event, the actions of King Arthur live on. The character was popularized in a 12th-cen-

---

THE IMAGINATION OF DON QUIXOTE, SHOWN HERE IN
19TH-CENTURY ARTWORK, TURNS A WINDMILL INTO A GIANT

tury book, *Historia Regum Britanniae* (*History of the Kings of Britain*), which quickly made the rounds among the literate British. In the story, King Arthur is served by the Knights of the Round Table, who sit in a circular fashion to demonstrate that none is superior. More recently, the tales surrounding King Arthur and the Knights of the Round Table were brought to life in the 1995 film *First Knight* and the 2004 film *King Arthur*.

King Arthur's tale isn't the only one that has made it to the big screen. *Ivanhoe* was turned into a 1952 movie featuring Elizabeth Taylor. The 2001 film *A Knight's Tale* puts a modern spin on classic knightly stories, with a soundtrack of modern rock classics set against a medieval English backdrop. The role of French knights during the Crusades was also dramatized in 2005's *Kingdom of Heaven*.

Although knights played an important part in history, at a time when rulers of small regions of Europe battled against each other in a bid for more territory and power, knightly battles complete with galloping horses, glinting swords, and chivalric behavior have receded into the past. Yet, tales of knights and the ideals they embodied—honor, bravery, courage, and loyalty—live on, on book pages and movie screens, at renaissance festivals, and, perhaps most of all, in our imaginations.

KING ARTHUR AND HIS KNIGHTS OF THE ROUND TABLE (ABOVE); A 12TH–CENTURY TEMPLAR KNIGHT (OPPOSITE)

Some groups of knights formed military orders, which had the purpose of crusading, or defending the Christian faith. The most famous military order was the Knights Templar, formed in 1118. Originally an order of French monastic knights, the Knights Templar patrolled roads in order to protect Christian pilgrims traveling to the Holy Land. Because the Knights Templar was an exclusive and secretive organization, rumors persist to this day about its actions. For example, the knights are often believed to have hidden the Holy Grail, the cup Jesus reportedly drank from during the Last Supper, and are featured in Dan Brown's popular novel The Da Vinci Code.

GLOSSARY

Bohemian—Someone from Bohemia, a region of central Europe located in the western and central parts of what is today the Czech Republic

catapults—Throwing mechanisms that launched objects over a wall or other barrier with great force

Celts—A people from mainland Europe who eventually settled on the islands of Britain and Ireland

central government—A government, usually based in a capital city, that makes decisions for the whole country, instead of letting regional governments make their own laws

chain mail—A protective suit worn by knights; chain mail suits consisted of thousands of tiny metal hoops linked meticulously together

earl—A title meaning "chief"; it was bestowed upon nobles by kings and passed down from generation to generation

heresy—Speaking against one's religion or religious rules, a charge often leveled by the Catholic Church during the Middle Ages

Holy Land—Modern-day Israel and Palestine, an area important to three major world religions (Christianity, Islam, and Judaism) as the home of ancient religious figures

jousting—Fighting with lances while on horseback; jousting was a knight's preferred method of battle during tournaments

longbows—Weapons made from a long, arched piece of wood and a bowstring; longbows were held vertically to launch arrows

manor—The land, and everything on it, owned by a lord; a manor might hold a castle, several homes, barns, stables, and buildings such as a blacksmith shop

martyr—A person who either suffers or dies while upholding his or her principles, usually in a religious context

medieval—A person, place, or thing from the Middle Ages or that embodies characteristics commonly found during the Middle Ages

mercenaries—Professional fighters who worked for whichever lord paid them the most money; they were not tied to the land, so they could fight for as long as necessary

Middle Ages—Roughly the time period between A.D. 400 and 1500 in Europe, starting with the decline of the Roman Empire and ending with the Protestant Reformation

moral—Having to do with principles of right and wrong, especially relating to the teaching of proper behavior and living through good conduct

nobles—Important people who ranked high within society; often they were wealthy, well-respected, and came from a long line of nobility

plunder—Another word for steal; to take goods and treasures by force or violence, often causing damage to the surroundings in the process

Prussian—Someone from the province of Prussia, a region that comprised modern-day northern Poland and northern Germany

ransom—Money or other items or conditions demanded in exchange for the release of hostages

rivets—Small pieces of metal used to hold together two larger pieces and hammered on each end to form a flattened head

Roman Empire—The vast empire, centered in Rome, that included most of modern-day Europe, Asia Minor, and northern Africa; the Roman Empire lasted from the eighth century B.C. to A.D. 476

romanticized—Thought of in a positive, romantic, or idealized way, often ignoring negative qualities

Saxons—A people from the German region of Saxony; the Saxons invaded Britain in the fourth century

siege—To attack a fort or castle by surrounding it and threatening the people inside until they are forced to surrender

Trughtbek.

Batyrton

50

Hillothby

hoghton.

INDEX

BIBLIOGRAPHY

Armstrong, Catherine. "William Marshal: Earl of Pembroke." The Castles of Wales. http://www.castlewales.com/marshall.html

Beltz, George Frederick. "Edward the Black Prince." Britannia Biographies. http://www.britannia.com/bios/royals/blckprnc.html

Britannia. "Henry II." Britannia Monarchs. http://www.britannia.com/history/monarchs/mon26.html

Buehr, Walter. *Knights and Castles and Feudal Life.* New York: G. P. Putnam's Sons, 1957.

Gravett, Christopher. *The Knight's Handbook.* New York: Cobblehill Books, 1997.

Public Broadcasting System. "Warrior Challenge: Knight." Public Broadcasting System. http://www.pbs.org/wnet/warriorchallenge/knights/time.html

Tanaka, Shelley. *In the Time of Knights.* Toronto: Hyperion/Madison Press, 2000.

University of Rochester. "King Arthur." The Camelot Project at the University of Rochester. http://www.lib.rochester.edu/camelot/cphome.stm